# Contents

Skills Grid
Introduction
| | | |
|---|---|---|
| Section A | Birthday maths | 1 |
| Section B | Rhymes | 5 |
| Section C | Counting songs | 9 |
| Section D | Register maths | 14 |
| Section E | Keep-fit maths | 18 |
| Section F | Numbers and counting | 21 |
| Section G | Story maths | 29 |
| Section H | Family maths | 32 |
| Section I | Money maths | 36 |
| Section J | Picture maths | 43 |

# Skills Grid

This grid shows the list of key skills covered by the activities in this book. The *Number* Teacher Cards make reference to these skills. For each skill, the most appropriate activities are identified.

| Skill | Activity |
|---|---|
| **1 Counting** | |
| 1.1 To recite the number names in order to 10/20/30 and back | A1, B5, B6, C2, C6, C8, D3, D8, E1, E2, E3, E4, F13, G1, G5, H1, H3, I7, I14, J3, J4, J5 |
| 1.2 To recite the number names in order to 40+ and back | F5 |
| 1.3 To recite the number names in order to 100 and back | I9 |
| 1.4 To recite the number names in order, counting on from a given number | B2 |
| 1.5 To recite the number names in order, counting back from a given number | B1, B3, B8, C1, C3, C4, C5, C7 |
| 1.6 To recognise written numerals up to 6/9/10/20 | E6, E7, E8, F1, F2, F3, F4, F6, F8, F10, F14, H2, H3, H6, H8 |
| 1.7 To recognise none or zero in the context of stories or rhymes | B1, B8, C7 |
| 1.8 To count reliably in contexts such as sounds (hand claps) or movements (hops) | A7, E3, E4, F1, F2, F6, F7, F9, F14 |
| 1.9 To count in multiples of ten | I5, I9, I10 |
| 1.10 To count in twos | B4, B6, F10, I5, I7, I9, I10 |
| **2 Comparing and ordering numbers** | |
| 2.1 To compare two given numbers using 'less than' and 'more than' | A8, D1, D2, D3, D4, D5, D7, D9, F1, F2, F9, F12, H1 |
| 2.2 To compare more than two numbers to a given number | D2, D4, H4 |
| 2.3 To suggest numbers which lie between two given numbers | A3, F5, F11, J6 |
| 2.4 To recognise ordinal number names | A1 |

| Skill | Activity |
|---|---|
| 2.5 To order consecutive numbers given in random order (e.g. 5, 3, 1, 2, 4) | A3, A6, E5, F3, F6, F10 |
| 2.6 To order any set of four or five numbers given in random order (e.g. 3, 1, 6, 7) | A3, F6, F11, F12, G5 |
| **3 Addition and subtraction** | |
| 3.1 To say one more than a given number | A4, A5, D6, D8, G2, G3, H5, H6, H7 |
| 3.2 To say one less than a given number | A4, C1, C3, C4, C5, C7, D6, G4, G6, H5, H6, H7, I7, I10, I13 |
| 3.3 To say two or three more than a given number | A5, D6, G3, H5, H7 |
| 3.4 To add by counting on | D8, G2, H7 |
| 3.5 To find a total when one set of objects is hidden | G6, H4 |
| 3.6 To partition a number of objects into two groups | B2, D7, I2 |
| 3.7 To select two groups to make a given total | I11, H5 |
| **4 Reasoning about numbers** | |
| 4.1 To recognise and recreate patterns | B5, B7, F7 |
| 4.2 To solve simple mathematical puzzles | A4, A5, A6, D7, G2, G3, G4, G6, H6, I12, I13, J1, J2 |
| 4.3 To make simple predictions involving numbers | A5, A6, F9, J1, J2 |
| **5 Problems involving money** | |
| 5.1 To recognise coins | I1, I2, I3, I5 |
| 5.2 To use coins in role play, paying and giving change | I4, I6, I8, I11 |
| **6 Time** | |
| 6.1 To recognise and begin to chant days of the week in order | D4 |
| 6.2 To begin to recognise months | A1, A2 |

# Introduction

The Mental Warm-up Activities provide a comprehensive scheme of work for developing mental mathematics strategies. The daily activities have been written to practise key mental maths skills, including counting, comparing and ordering numbers, addition and subtraction facts etc.

## How to use this book

Every day, before the main part of the lesson, select an appropriate activity from this book. The activities are designed to rehearse and sharpen key skills, and will allow you to get off to a clear, crisp start to the lesson.

To allow the teacher flexibility, the book is arranged under topic headings, e.g. Birthday maths, Rhymes, Counting songs etc. On the back of each *Number* Teacher Card, reference is made to appropriate skills covered in this book. These skills are outlined on page ii in the Skills Grid, and for each skill a list of the most appropriate activities is given. For each *Number* Unit, the teacher will need to check the relevant skills on the back of the Teacher Card, then refer to the Skills Grid to decide which particular activities to use.

Many of the activities practice 'basic' skills such as counting, but there is plenty of variety throughout this book to give the teacher a wide choice of formats and styles. Of course, some of the activities will become favourites that you and the children will want to return to throughout the year.

### Shape, Space and Measures

The *Shape, Space and Measures* Teacher Cards do not make reference to specific skills covered by this book. When teaching the *Shape, Space and Measures* Units, it is an ideal opportunity to go back and rehearse some key skills, in particular focusing on counting. You will need to plan which activities (or skills) you need to cover Unit by Unit, and this will vary, depending on the time of year, the stage of the children etc. The Skills Grid on page ii provides invaluable assistance in this planning.

# Section A: Birthday maths

## A1 Which month?

*To begin to recognise months; to recite the number names in order to 31; to recognise ordinal number names*

Ask the children *Do you know the date of your birthday? Can you say the number and the month?* (e.g. the 15th of April).
Say *Let's count up to Jane's birth date: 1, 2, 3, 4 … 15 STOP!*
*Now let's try the months. Start at January. January, February, March, April. STOP!*
*How many months was that? Try it again together.*
*Four altogether; so it's not the first, not the second, not the third, but the FOURTH month.*
Encourage the children to join in.

## A2 Birthday train

*To begin to recognise months*

Make a large display of a train in which the engine and each carriage represents a different month.

Ask each child to draw a picture of him or herself, and put it on the carriage matching their birthday.

Ask questions about the train.
*Who is in the first carriage? What month is Jo's carriage?*

## A3 Who is the oldest?

*To suggest numbers which lie between two given numbers; to order consecutive numbers given in random order; to order any set of four or five numbers given in random order*

**Collection of toy animals wearing birthday badges ('I am 3', 'I am 5', 'I am 6', 'I am 7')**

Pull out the toy with the 'I am 3' sticker on it, and ask a child to hold it. *How old is this toy?*

Pull out another one. *Is this one older or younger than the first?*

Continue with the other toys, putting them in order, youngest to oldest. *Which number is missing? Where should it go?* Ask a four-year-old (if you have one) to put him or herself in the correct place in the line.

## A4 I know a little girl (or boy) ...

*To say one more than a given number; to say one less than a given number; to solve simple mathematical puzzles*

Ask the children *I know a little girl who is one year older than Jenny: how old is she?*

*I know a little boy who is one year younger than Sean: how old is he?*

Can children put themselves with other children the same age once a few of them have answered the questions?

Repeat the activity, but this time using two/three years older/younger.

## A5 Which class?

*To say one or two more than a given number; to solve simple mathematical puzzles; to make simple predictions involving numbers*

Ask the children *If you are five years old now, how old will you be in one year/two years from now? Whose class will you be in then? Who has a younger brother or sister who will be in **this** class by then?*

## A6 How old are you?

*To order consecutive numbers given in random order; to solve simple mathematical puzzles; to make simple predictions involving numbers*

**Number cards (1 to 9), one set**

Give each of nine children one of the number cards 1 to 9. Place the child holding 1 on one side of the room, and the child holding 9 on the other.

Ask the other seven children to order themselves according to the number on their card.

Ask the rest of the children to say how old they are one by one, and to line up (sitting) in front of 'their' number (4 or 5).

*Which is the longest line? Who will be five next out of the four-year-olds? Do you know anyone (e.g. sister) who could go in front of 7?*

## A7 Happy birthday to you!

*To count reliably in contexts such as sounds (hand claps) or movements (hops)*

Whenever it is someone's birthday, sing 'Happy Birthday' to them, and follow by clapping the relevant number of claps. Count as you clap. Remember to STOP at the correct number.

You can have birthdays for the toys in your classroom, with varying ages from one to nine years.

Instead of claps, the children can hop or jump the number of years.

## A8 Mystery age

*To compare two given numbers using 'less than' and 'more than'*

Say to the children *It's my pet chicken's birthday today. Can you guess how old she is?*

The children make guesses and you answer with 'more/less' until they get the correct answer.

It might help to have an 'assistant' standing by the number line and pointing at the numbers suggested.

# Section B: Rhymes

## B1 Two birds

*To recite the number names in order, counting back from a given number; to recognise none or zero in the context of stories or rhymes*

> There were two birds
> Sitting on a stone.
> One flew away,
> Then there was one.
> The other flew after,
> Then were was none,
> And so the poor stone
> Was left all alone.

Use two children to act out the rhyme.

## B2 Eight magpies

*To recite the number names in order, counting on from a given number; to partition a number of objects into two groups*

> I saw eight magpies in a tree,
> Two for you and six for me.
> One for sorrow, two for mirth,
> Three for a wedding, four for a birth.
> Five for England, six for France,
> Seven for a fiddler, eight for a dance.

Use children to represent the magpies, emphasising the partition in the first verse.

## B3 Five little leaves

*To recite the number names in order, counting back from a given number*

> Five little leaves so bright and free
> Were dancing about one day on a tree.
> The wind came blowing through the town
> OOOOOOO ... OOOOOOO ...
> One little leaf came tumbling down.
>
> Four little leaves so bright and free, etc.

Use fingers to represent leaves.

## B4 Ten fat sausages

*To count in twos*

> Ten fat sausages sizzling in a pan,
> One went *Pop* and another went *Bang*.
>
> Eight fat sausages, etc.

Use fingers or children to represent sausages.

## B5 One, two, buckle my shoe

*To recite the number names in order to 20; to recognise and recreate patterns*

One, two, buckle my shoe,
Three, four, knock at the door.
Five, six, pick up sticks,
Seven, eight, don't be late.
Nine, ten, a big fat hen,
Eleven, twelve, dig and delve.
Thirteen, fourteen, maids a'courting,
Fifteen, sixteen, maids in the kitchen.
Seventeen, eighteen, maids in waiting,
Nineteen, twenty, my plate's empty!

## B6 One, two, three, four

*To recite the number names in order to 8; to count in twos*

One, two, three, four,
Mary at the cottage door.
Five, six, seven, eight,
Eating cherries off a plate.
Two, four, six, eight,
Mary at the cottage gate,
Eating cherries off a plate,
Two, four, six, eight.

## B7 Ten little squirrels

*To recognise and recreate patterns*

Ten little squirrels sat in a tree.
The first two said *Why, what do we see.*
The next two said *A man with a sack.*
The next two said *Get back, get back!*
The next two said *Let's hide in the shade.*
The next two said *Why, we're not afraid.*
But the sack looked big
So they ran away and hid!

Use fingers or ten children, in pairs, to act the rhyme.

## B8 Four little fish

*To recite the number names in order, counting back from a given number; to recognise none or zero in the context of stories or rhymes*

Four little fish swam out to sea,
One met a huge shark and then there were three.

Three little fish wondering what to do,
One hid in a great big shell and then there were two.

Two little fish looking for some fun,
One chased after a tiny wave and that left only one.

One little fish with all his friends gone,
Went back home to find his mum and that left none.

Use four children to represent the little fish and one to be their mum.

# Section C: Counting songs

## C1 Five currant buns

*To recite the number names in order, counting back from a given number; to say one less than a given number*

**Five cardboard cut-out 'buns' (or other objects), Blu-tack**

Five currant buns in the baker's shop,
Round and fat with sugar on the top.
Along came Ilesh with a penny one day
Bought a currant bun and took it away.

Four currant buns, etc.

No currant buns in the baker's shop,
Nothing round and fat with sugar on the top.
*Oh dear*, said the baker with the empty tray
*I'll have to make some more*, and he did it right away.

So there were, ...

Use five objects (or five children) to represent buns, or five cardboard buns stuck on to the board with Blu-tack. Use real coins if possible.

## C2 One, two, three, four, five

*To recite the number names in order to 10*
**Number cards (1 to 10), one set**

One, two, three, four, five
Once I caught a fish alive,
Six, seven, eight, nine, ten,
Then I let it go again.

Why did you let it go?
Because it bit my finger so.
Which finger did it bite?
This little finger on the right.

Ten children have number cards 1 to 10 and hold up the appropriate card as the song is being sung.

## ⬤3 Ten in the bed

*To recite the number names in order, counting back from a given number; to say one less than a given number*

There were ten in the bed and the little one said,
*Roll over! Roll over!*
So they all rolled over and one rolled out.

There were nine in the bed, etc.

Ten children stand up. They all turn around once on the words *So they all rolled over*. The child at the end of the line sits down on the words *and one fell out*.

## ⬤4 Ten green bottles

*To recite the number names in order, counting back from a given number; to say one less than a given number*

Ten green bottles hanging on the wall,
Ten green bottles hanging on the wall,
And if one green bottle should accidentally fall,
There'll be nine green bottles hanging on the wall.

Nine green bottles, etc.

Ten children stand in a row. One sits down on the words *Should accidentally fall*.

Alternatively, use ten cut-out cardboard bottles stuck to the board with Blu-tack, or ten green plastic bottles. These can be numbered.

## C5 Five little ducks

*To recite the number names in order, counting back from a given number; to say one less than a given number*

Five little ducks went swimming one day,
Over the pond and far away.
Mother duck said *Quack, quack, quack, quack*,
But only four little ducks came back.

Four little ducks, etc.

Last verse:

One little duck went swimming one day,
Over the pond and far away.
Mother duck said *Quack, quack, quack, quack*,
And five little ducks came swimming back.

Six children act out the song, or all the children use their fingers to represent the ducks.

## C6 One elephant went out to play

*To recite the number names in order to 10/20*

One elephant went out to play
Upon a spider's web one day.
He had such tremendous fun
That he called for another elephant to come.

Two elephants went out, etc.

Ten elephants went out to play
Upon a spider's web one day.
There were too many elephants having such fun.
That they fell through the web and then there were none.

One child represents the first elephant, then chooses another, etc.

## C7 Five little speckled frogs

*To recite the number names in order, counting back from a given number; to recognise none or zero in the context of stories or rhymes; to say one less than a given number*

Five little speckled frogs
Sat on a great big log,
Eating some most delicious bugs. Yum, yum!
One jumped into the pool,
Where it was nice and cool,
Then there were four green speckled frogs. Glub, glub!

Five children are frogs and act out the tale. Discuss how many on the log and how many in the pool.

## 8 One man went to mow

*To recite the number names in order to 10/20 and back*

One man went to mow,
Went to mow a meadow,
One man and his dog,
Went to mow a meadow.

Two men went to mow,
Went to mow a meadow
Two men, one man and his dog,
Went to mow a meadow.

Three men went to mow, etc.

# Section **D**: Register maths

## **D**1 School dinners

*To compare two given numbers using 'less than' and 'more than'*

Ask how many of the children have school dinners, and how many have packed lunches.

Compare the two numbers. *Are there more packed lunches than school dinners? How many more/less?*

## **D**2 More school dinners

*To compare two given numbers using 'less than' and 'more than'; to compare more than two numbers to a given number*
**Beads, string**

On a string, record with beads all the children who have school dinners.

On a second string, record with beads all those who have packed lunches.

If there are any home dinners, put beads for them on a third string.

Count the beads on each string and compare them.

Ask questions about how many more/less each string has.

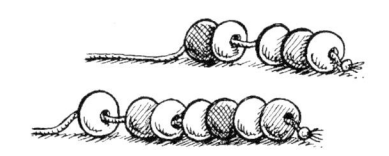

## D3 Daily attendance

*To compare two given numbers using 'less than' and 'more than'; to recite the number names in order to 30*

Discuss the daily attendance.
*How many children are in our class?*
*How many children are in class today?*
*How many children are absent?*
*If there were 2 children away yesterday, is the number absent today more or less than yesterday?*
If all children are present, it's a 'Full House'.

## D4 Absent friends

*To compare two given numbers using 'less than' and 'more than'; to compare more than two numbers to a given number; to recognise and begin to chant days of the week in order*

Keep a record of absences throughout week: Monday 2; Tuesday 3; etc.

Stand children up to represent these daily totals.

Discuss the totals. *On which day were most children away? Which day had most children here?* etc.

## **D** 5 What's in a name?

*To compare two given numbers using 'less than' and 'more than'*

Look at the letters in the children's names.

Stand up all the children with three/four/five/six letters, etc.

Count how many children have four letters in their name.

Now count the children with six letters in their names. *Are there more or less? How many more/less?*

## **D** 6 More or less?

*To say one more than a given number; to say one less than a given number; to say two or three more than a given number*

Choose a child and ask the class *How many letters does Yoichi have in his name?*

Ask the child if the class is correct.

Ask the children to stand up/kneel/put their hands up if their name has one/two/three more letters than the chosen name.

Repeat for names with one/two/three letters less than the chosen name.

## D7 Boys and girls

*To compare two given numbers using 'less than' and 'more than'; to solve simple mathematical puzzles; to partition a number of objects into two groups*

Discuss the number of boys and girls in class.
*How many girls are there in class today?*
*How many boys are there in class today?*
*Are there more girls than boys?*
*Are there more boys than girls?*
*Can we find the difference?*

## D8 Counting round the class

*To say one more than a given number; to recite the number names in order to 10/20 and back; to add by counting on*

When calling out the register ask the children to count around the class. The first child says *One*, the second child says *Two*, etc. until everyone has said a number. Emphasise that this final number is how many children are in the class that day.

This can also be done to count the children on each table or in each group, the number of boys and the number of girls.

## D9 Alphabet names

*To compare two given numbers using 'less than' and 'more than'*

Ask the class *How many children's names begin with A?*
*How many begin with B?*
*How many more/less begin with A than with B?* etc.
This activity can be done with forenames or surnames.

# Section **E**: Keep-fit maths

For all the activities in this sections the children need to sit or stand in their own space, with enough room to stretch out their arms or jump. Many of the activities are suitable for use during 'hall time'.

## **E**1 Fives and tens

*To recite the number names in order to 10*

The children start with their arms by their sides. Count aloud in unison up to five: One, two, three, four, five! On 'five' the children shoot our one arm with five fingers stretched out. Continue the count up to ten. On 'ten' the children shoot out the other arm, and wave ten fingers in the air. They place their arms back by their sides, and continue to 20.

## **E**2 Teens numbers

*To recite the number names in order to 20*

The children sit on the floor with their knees pulled up, and arms folded. Count aloud in unison, with the children holding up fingers to match the numbers. On 'ten' they shoot out both feet, and fold down their fingers. Now continue up to 20, with two feet and one finger matching 11, two feet and two fingers matching 12, etc.

## **E**3 Jumping jacks

*To recite the number names in order to 10; to count reliably in contexts such as sound or movements*

Use a large set of number cards (1 to 10). Hide a card behind your back. Say *Ready, steady go*, and reveal the card. The children shout the number aloud and jump a matching number of times.

Repeat until all the cards have been used.

## E4 Hopping mad

*To recite the number names in order to 10/20; to count reliably in contexts such as sound or movements*

Choose a child to stand at the front and hop on one leg, slowly. The rest of the class count the hops. When the first child stops, agree with the class the number of hops. Give the first child a matching number card. Choose a new child to be the 'hopper'.

Who can hop the most times?

## E5 Line up

*To order consecutive numbers given in random order*
**Number cards (1 to 10 or 20)**

Give each child a number card (several children may have each number). Ask the children to form a line as you say their number: One, two, three, …

When all the children are in a line, say: Scatter, and the children start to run around. After a few moments say: Line, and all the children line up in order as quickly as possible (you may have to count to help them).

Repeat.

## E6 Bean bag count

*To recognise written numerals up to 9*
**Number cards (1 to 9), a bean bag**

Give each child a number card to hold (or pin it to their front). Each child walks around slowly. Say a number and throw a bean bag to the child with the matching number card. They say another number and throw the bean bag to a child with that number card. Continue.

## E7 Musical numbers

*To recognise written numerals up to 6*
**Sets of number cards (1 to 6), a dice**

Give each child a number card to hold (or pin it to their front). Play some music, to which the children walk around. Stop the music and the children have to 'freeze'. Roll the dice and call out the number. Any child with that number is 'out' and stands to one side. Start the music again, and continue, until all the children are 'out'.

## E8 Stop and go

*To recognise written numerals up to 10 (or 20)*
**Number cards (1 to 10 or 20)**

Give each child a number card to hold (or pin it to their front). The children stand, well spaced-out. Say a number. All the children with that number run around, weaving in and out of the other children. Say *Stop*, and all the children stand still again. Say a new number, and those children run around. Continue.

# Section F: Numbers and counting

## F1 Silly Teddy

*To recognise written numerals up to 9; to count reliably in contexts such as sounds (hand claps) or movements (hops); to compare two given numbers using 'less than' and 'more than'*
**A teddy bear, number line (0 to 9)**

Hold Silly Teddy in front of the class and explain that sometimes he gets muddled. *We are going to help Teddy find the right number.*

Choose a child and whisper a number in his or her ear. The child then has to drum/hit/clap the appropriate number of beats.

Then move Silly Teddy to a wrong number on the number line. The children have to shout out *More!* or *Less!* and Teddy moves along the number line one place at a time according to what the children shout.

## F2 Silly Teddy (marbles)

*To recognise written numerals up to 9; to count reliably in contexts such as sounds (hand claps) or movements (hops); to compare two given numbers using 'less than' and 'more than'*
**A teddy bear, marbles, a bag, number line (0 to 9)**

Put some marbles in a bag. Ask one of the children to pull out a handful of marbles and to count them silently, dropping them slowly back into the bag while they count, so that the class can see.

Teddy listens too, and puts himself next to the wrong number on the number line. Children shout out *More!* or *Less!* and Teddy moves up or down the number line.

## F3 Bossyboot numbers

*To recognise written numerals up to 9; to order consecutive numbers given in random order.*
**Number cards (0 to 9)**

Give ten children a number card each and line them up 'in a muddle'.

The other children act as the 'Bossyboots', calling out instructions to one child at a time to put them in the correct order, e.g. *Jade, you need to move to the end of the line next to Latha* and *Jack, can you go and stand between Sonja and Jyoti?*

Children who find it difficult to say the instructions could come up and gently move children.

## F4 What's my number?

*To recognise written numerals up to 9*
**Wooden/plastic numbers**

Choose children to come up to the front one by one. Turn them to face the other children, with their back to you.

Choose a number between 0 and 9 and 'draw' the number slowly and deliberately on their back with your finger, so that they can feel your finger tracing the outline. Can they guess what the number is?

Give them some help *It's got a round part, and a straight line right next to it* (9). *It's got a hook, and then a straight line across the bottom* (2).

If you have wooden/plastic numbers, the children can hold the number behind their back and feel it.

## F 5 Silly Teddy (counting problems)

*To recite the number names in order to 40 and back; to suggest numbers which lie between two given numbers; to solve simple mathematical puzzles*
**A teddy bear**

Tell the children that Silly Teddy has been learning to count and that you want them to listen to see how well he is doing.

You count for Teddy, stumbling and hesitating after a few numbers, e.g. *One, two, three… four, five, six, seven …eight, nine …ten, eleven, twelve, fourteen, fifteen, sixteen …*

*Oh no, Teddy missed out a number. Let's start from 10 and count with Teddy. Ten, eleven … twenty.*

*Which number did Teddy miss out?*

Repeat, missing out other numbers.

Repeat, but counting back from 10 or 20.

## F 6 Musical numbers

*To recognise written numerals up to 9; to count reliably in contexts such as sounds (hand claps) or movements (hops); to order any set of four or five numbers given in random order; to order consecutive numbers given in random order*
**A tape player; a music tape; a bag; small number cards (1 to 20), one set**

Put the number cards in a bag. Then sit everyone in a circle and play the music. The children pass the bag of numbers around the circle as the music plays.

When the music stops, the child holding the bag removes a card from the bag and reads it out. Can they hop that number of times? Then the number is placed in the middle of the circle on the floor. As more numbers are placed in the middle of the circle, encourage children to place them in the correct order, to create a number line.

## ❼ 7 Clap, clap!

*To count reliably in contexts such as sounds (hand claps) or movements (hops); to recognise and recreate patterns*

This is a useful activity to use at any time for attracting attention quickly without having to use your voice. If you are using it for the first time, or getting the children used to it, it is best to use it as a carpet-time activity.

Clap a simple pattern to the children, such as clap, clap, clap – (pause) – clap, clap, clap – (pause).

Ask them to listen and then to join in with the pattern.

Once all the children can join in with your clapping satisfactorily, ask them to describe the pattern. They may come up with various ways to describe the same pattern, e.g. *It's six claps with a rest in the middle* or *It's three, stop, three, stop*.

As children get better at listening and copying, introduce more complicated patterns, such as clap, clap, slap (on lap), click (fingers), which creates a 2, 1, 1, pattern.

## **F** 8 The postman game

*To recognise written numerals up to 9; to count reliably in contexts such as sounds (hand claps) or movements (hops)*

**Six Post-it notes with numbers up to 20 written on them; a 'post bag' with old envelopes (about 40) in it; a woodblock (or anything else to make a knocking sound)**

Sit the children in a circle with enough space around them for a child to walk around. Stick the Post-it notes on the backs of six chosen children, hidden from them.

Choose one child to be the postman. Give her the bag and the woodblock. She walks around the circle, randomly choosing the children with numbers on their backs and 'delivering the post'.

The postman knocks on the door the same number of times as the number on the door. So if the number on the Post-It note is 9, the postman knocks nine times.

The child counts the number of knocks, turns to the postman and says *Hello, do I have 9 letters today?*

The postman answers *Yes* or *No* and gives the child the correct number of letters, counting out loud as she passes the letters over. This gives children who did not get it correct first time a second chance.

## **F** 9 Please, Mrs Gatelady

*To compare two given numbers using 'less than' and 'more than'; to make simple predictions involving numbers; to partition a set into two groups*

**A hoop or large circle; number cards (0 to 9, or 10 to 20), two or three sets**

Sit the children in a circle and place the hoop in the middle.

Deal a card to every child. Explain that you are Mrs Gatelady/Mr Gateman and that you are in charge of this field (the hoop). You only let certain numbers into your field, but your reason is secret.

Give the children a few examples, such as 'Numbers more than 5', 'Numbers less than 10' and explain that the reason will change every time you play the game.

To play the game, each child shows his or her card to you and says *Please Mrs Gatelady/Mr Gateman, may I come in?* You look at the card and answer *Yes, you may* or *No, you may not*. The children place their card outside or inside the hoop accordingly.

As more children place their card, it will become more obvious what the 'secret' is. Ask the children to keep the secret until everyone has had their go. Can they guess what your secret was?

This activity also works well for sorting shapes.

## ❿ 10 Activities with a number line

*To recognise written numerals up to 9; to count in twos; to order consecutive numbers given in random order*

### A number line (1 to 20)

- Mix up the numbers and ask the children to reorder them.

- Display numbers with odd numbers on one side and even on the other.
  *Count in twos, starting at 1.*
  *Count in twos, starting at 2.*

- Place several numbers upside down and ask the children to spot the deliberate mistake.

- Give each number to one of the children and ask them to arrange themselves in the correct order. Ask questions like *Which number comes before 4? Who is holding that number? Which number comes after number 4? Who has that number?*

- Have a number line on the floor. This can be in the shape of the children's feet. As they line up, they can see and talk about the numbers.

## F11 A daily challenge

*To suggest numbers which lie between two given numbers; to order any set of four or five numbers given in random order*

Give the children a daily challenge. For example:
*Fill in my missing number: 37, ..., 39*
*Put these numbers in order: 45, 51, 40, 49*
*Put these numbers in order: 10, 40, 20, 30*

## F12 Order, order!

*To compare two given numbers using 'less than' and 'more than'; to order any set of four or five numbers given in random order*

**Number cards (1 to 20)**

Hold up a number and ask the children to name it.

Then ask for a child for any number less than that/more than that.

Either the child saying the number or the teacher could write the number on the board.

Then the numbers can be put in order.

## F13 Write a counting rhyme

*To recite the number names in order to 10*

In the literacy hour, when looking at nursery rhymes, encourage the children to write their own counting rhymes. For example:

One, two, three, four, five,
How many bees live in that hive?
Six, seven, eight, nine, ten,
I'm not counting them again!

## F14 Counting echoes

*To recognise written numerals up to 9; to count reliably in other contexts such as sound (hand claps) or movements (hops)*

**Number cards (0 to 9), one set**

Deal a card at random to a child, who reads the number aloud and claps to match.

The other children echo the claps.

Then everyone checks the card to see if they were correct.

# Section G: Story maths

## G1 Tell me a story

*To recite the number names in order to 10*
**Sets of number cards (1 to 6 or 10)**

Give each child a number card. Explain that you are going to tell a story, and that each time you say a number, the children with the matching card must stand up. They will need to listen carefully. Begin the story: **One** *day* … all the children with '1' should stand up. Continue: **One** *day*, **six** *dogs went for a walk* …

Continue the story, including appropriate numbers, until all the children are standing.

## G2 Story puzzle

*To add by counting on; to say two or three more than a given number; to solve simple mathematical puzzles*

Explain that you are going to tell a story that is really a puzzle. The answer is a number and the children will have to listen very carefully.

*Once upon a time there was a boy with three bossy sisters. He got fed up with being told what to do all the time, so one night he put a banana in each of their school bags. The bananas made a squishy mess all over his sister's books and they were very cross. The boy thought it was funny and ate another banana to celebrate.*

How many bananas were in the story?

Take some suggestions, then re-tell the story, holding up a finger for each banana.

## G3 Imagine a ...

*To say one more than a given number; to say two or three more than a given number; to solve simple mathematical puzzles*

Tell the children to shut their eyes and imagine an elephant walking around a zoo. It is a Mummy elephant, and soon she meets her three children, one big, one medium and one small. How many elephants altogether?

Re-tell the story, with the children holding up a finger to match each elephant.

Play again, with different animals. Encourage the children to think of their own stories.

## G4 Magic carpet

*To say one less than a given number; to solve simple mathematical puzzles*

Tell the children a story.

*One child goes for a ride on a magic carpet, and decides to take two friends with him. Unfortunately one of his friends falls off the carpet. Luckily he lands in a pile of hay, so he is alright. But how many children are still on the carpet?*

Take some suggestions, then choose three children to act out the story. Repeat for different numbers of children. Only one child falls off each time.

## G5 Out of order

*To order any set of four or five numbers given in random order; to recite the number names to 10*
**Number line (1 to 10)**

Remove four cards at random from the line. Tell the children a story.

*At night the number cards come alive, get down from the line and play. Some of them are very naughty and won't go back in the right place.*

Show the four number cards. We have to help put these back in the right place. Ask the children which is smallest. Then the next smallest, etc. Place the four cards in order then choose children to help you replace them on the line.

## G6 Gold pieces

*To say one more or less than a given number; to solve simple mathematical puzzles; to find a total when one set of objects is hidden*

*Once upon a time a prince and princess went on a long journey, with ten gold pieces.* Choose two children to be the prince and princess and give them a bag with ten counters.

*The prince and princess were walking through a wood when they say a woodcutter who was sitting, crying. When they asked him why, he said he had no money to buy food for his family. So the kind prince and princess gave him one of their gold pieces …*

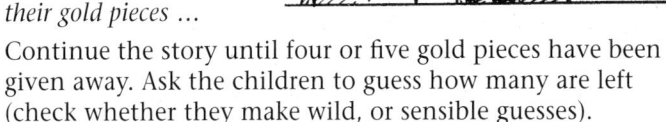

Continue the story until four or five gold pieces have been given away. Ask the children to guess how many are left (check whether they make wild, or sensible guesses).

Count the remaining gold pieces to check.

Repeat the story, this time with the children collecting gold pieces and adding them to their bag.

# Section H: Family maths

## H1 Compare two families

*To recite the number names in order to 10; to compare two given numbers using 'less than' and 'more than'*
**A carpet square, four soft toy bears**

Put a bear 'family' on a carpet square (e.g. a family of four bears). Ask the children to count the bears with you.

Then ask each child in turn whether their own family has more, fewer or the same number of people as the bear family.

Change the size of the bear family and repeat.

## H2 How many in your family?

*To recognise written numerals up to 9*
**A carpet square, number cards (0 to 9), one set**

Place number cards from 2 to 9 on a carpet square.

Ask each child, in turn, to name the members of their family and hold up the matching number of fingers.

Then ask the children to find the number card showing the number of people in their family.

Alternatively, hold up the number cards 2 to 9 in random order and ask the children to stand up if the card shows the number of people in their family.

## H3 Number the bears

*To recognise written numerals up to 9; to recite the number names in order to 9*
**Compare bears (or 'families' of toy animals), carpet squares, number cards (1 to 9), one set**

Make several bear families on the carpet squares. Place the number cards 1 to 9 around the carpet squares at random.

Ask the children to choose the correct number card to label each bear family.

Now label the families incorrectly and ask the children to rearrange the cards so that each family is correctly labelled again.

Alternatively, put number cards at random on the carpet squares and ask the children to put the correct number of bears on each square.

## H4 Compare bear families

*To compare more than two numbers to a given number; to find a total when one set of objects is hidden*
**Compare bears (or similar 'sorting' objects), carpet squares**

Make bear families of 2 to 9 bears on the carpet squares.

Ask the children to identify which of the bear families has the same number of members as their family.

Choose two bear families and place one in a bag. Can the children say how many in total? Repeat for different families.

## H5 Add or subtract

*To say one more/one less than a given number; to say two or three more than a given number; to select two groups to make a given total*
**A carpet square, Compare bears (or similar 'sorting' objects), number cards (0 to 9), one set**

Make a bear family on a carpet square.

Now ask the children to add or subtract bears until the bear family has the same number of members as their own family.

## H6 One more, one less

*To recognise written numerals up to 9; to say one more/one less than a given number; to solve simple mathematical puzzles*
**A carpet square, Compare bears (or similar 'sorting' objects), number cards (0 to 9)**

Put a bear family on a carpet square and label it with the appropriate number card.

Tell the children 'one more' stories, such as *Mummy bear has a baby* and *Grandma bear comes to stay*. Ask the children to say how many bears are in the family now and to change the label to show the new number in the family.

Now tell the children 'one less' stories, such as *Three bears are having dinner; one finishes and leaves the table* and *Five bears are watching the television; Daddy bear goes to have a bath*. As before, ask the children to say how many bears are in the family now and to change the label.

## H7 Build a tower

*To say one more/one less than a given number; to say two or three more than a given number; to add by counting on*
**Interlocking cubes**

Ask one child to make an interlocking tower equal to the number of members in his or her family.

That child then passes it to the next, who adds or subtracts cubes, or leaves it unchanged, according to the size of his or her family.

Continue passing the tower round the class until everyone has had a turn.

## H8 Match the card

*To recognise written numerals up to 9*
**Number cards (0 to 9), one set**

Ask the children to show how many there are in their families by holding up the appropriate number of fingers.

Hold up the number cards at random. Ask the children to stand up if the number on the card corresponds to the number in their family – and therefore also the number of fingers they are holding up.

# Section 1: Money maths

## 1.2 Compare coins

*To recognise coins*
**Real 1p, 2p, 5p, 10p coins, one per child**

Give each child a coin.

Ask the children to look for the head. Ask if anyone knows whose head it is. Discuss other pictures on the coins.

Then ask the children to turn over their coin. *What is the value of the coin?*

Pair the children and ask them to compare their coins. Discuss with them whose coin is worth more/less, or are they the same?

## 1.2 Copper and silver

*To partition a number of objects into two groups; to recognise coins*
**Two sorting rings; labels saying 'brown' and 'silver'; real 1p, 2p, 5p, 10p coins, one per child**

Give each child a coin. Discuss the colours.

Place two sorting rings on the table or floor, and label them 'brown' and 'silver'. Invite each child to place his or her coin in the appropriate ring.

Discuss the values of the coins in each set.

## ❶3 Coin values

*To recognise coins*
**1p, 2p, 5p, 10p coins, one per child**

Give each child a coin.

Ask one child to tell you the value of his or her coin. Ask others who have a coin of the same value to put up their hands.

Repeat for the other values.

Discuss the values for which there are no coins, e.g. 3p, 4p, 6p.

## ❶4 How many pennies?

*To use coins in role play, paying and giving change*
**Toys clearly labelled with prices, 1p to 10p; 1p coins; a bag**

Put the toys on the floor. Pass round the bag of coins while chanting the following rhyme, or something similar:

> We're going to buy a toy,
> We're going to the shops.
> Take the money from the bag
> When the bag stops.

When the chant finishes, the child holding the bag takes out the correct number of 1p coins to pay for a toy of his or her choice.

## ❶5 Match the card

*To recognise coins; to count in twos; to count in multiples of ten*
**1p, 2p, 5p, 10p coins, one per child; 1p, 2p, 5p, 10p cards**

Place the cards on the floor. Give each child a coin (or pass a bag of coins round).

Ask each child in turn to put his or her coin on the appropriate card.

Count the 1p coins in ones, the 2p coins in twos, the 5p coins in fives and the 10p coins in tens.

## ❶6 Pairs of toys

*To use coins in role play, paying and giving change*
**Toys clearly labelled with prices, 1p to 10p; 1p coins; a purse or pot**

Put two toys with price labels on the floor.

Put 1p coins to the total value of the two toys in the purse or pot.

Ask a child to take out the exact amount for one of the toys.

Ask another child to take out the exact amount for the second toy. Discuss what is left in the purse.

Repeat with further pairs of toys of different total value.

## ❶7 Out of the bag

*To say one less than a given number; to recite the number names in order to 20 and back; to count in twos*
**1p coins; a bag**

Count 1p coins into the bag with the children, so that they know how many coins it contains.

Pass the bag round the class. Each child takes 1p out of the bag, while the others have to say how much is left in the bag. Continue until the bag is empty.

Repeat the activity, starting with a different number of coins and continuing until all the children have had a turn.

**Extension** – take out two 1p coins each time.

## ❶8 Can you buy this toy?

*To use coins in role play, paying and giving change*
**Toys clearly labelled with prices, 1p to 10p; 1p, 2p, 5p, 10p coins; a bag**

Put the toys on the floor. Put the coins in a bag and give the bag to a child. The children pass the bag of coins around, while chanting:

> Can you buy this toy?
> Can you buy this toy?
> How much money do you have?
> Can you buy this toy?

Then, targeting the children according to their ability, hold up a toy and ask questions such as:

*Do you have enough money? The exact amount? Not enough?*

*Does it cost more than you have?*

*Can you buy it and get some change?*

## ● 9 Into the pot

*To recite the number names in order to 100 and back; to count in twos; to count in multiples of ten*
**1p, 2p and 10p coins; a pot or hat**

Give each child a 1p coin. Give the empty pot to a child.

The children pass the pot around, each putting in his or her 1p coin. As each coin goes in, all the children chant the total in the pot.

Repeat with 2p coins, counting in twos. (You could stop at 20p and start again.) Repeat with 10p coins, counting in tens. When you get to 100p, tell the children that 100p = £1. Start again and continue until all the children have put their coins in the pot. Reverse the activity, counting back from 100p and removing the coins from the pot as you do so.

## ● 10 Out of the pot

*To say one less than a given number; to count in twos; to count in multiples of ten*
**1p, 2p, 10 coins; a pot**

Count ten 1p coins into the pot and give it to a child.

The children pass the pot around, each taking out a 1p coin. As each coin comes out, all the children chant how much remains in the pot.

Repeat with ten 2p coins in the pot (or extend to twenty 2p coins), counting back in twos.

Repeat with five 10p coins in the pot (or extend to ten 10p coins), counting back in tens.

## ❶ 11 The right money

*To use coins in role play, paying and giving change; to select two groups to make a given total*
**Toys clearly labelled with prices, 1p, 2p, 5p, 10p; 1p, 2p, 5p, 10p coins; a bag**

Put the toys on the carpet. Put the coins in the bag and give it to a child.

The children pass the bag around, each taking out the correct money to buy a toy of his or her choice.

Encourage the children to explore taking two 1p coins or one 2p coin to pay for a toy priced at 2p, etc.

Extend by choosing a toy and asking children to find different ways of making the correct amount.

## ❶ 12 Think of a toy

*To solve simple mathematical puzzles involving money*
**Toys clearly labelled with prices, 1p to 10p**

Put the toys on the carpet. Think of a toy and give the children clues to help them identify it. For example:

*This toy can be bought with a 1p coin and a 2p coin.*

*This toy costs 1p less/more than that toy* (indicating appropriately).

*This toy can be bought with a 5p coin and a 1p coin.*

*In my purse I have only 4p. The toy I am thinking of costs 1p more.*

Encourage the children to take the role of the teacher and to *Think of a toy*.

# ⬤13 How much is left?

*To say one less than a given number; to solve simple mathematical puzzles involving money*

Ask the children to imagine that they have 5p in their purses. Tell stories like these:

*You spend 1p on a sweet. How much will you have left?*
*You spend 2p on a comic. How much will you have left?*
*You spend 3p on a balloon. How much do you have now?*

Extend to 10p. Encourage the children to use their fingers to represent the total in the purse.

# ⬤14 How much for this?

*To recite the number names to 10*
**£1 coins**

Draw a picture on the board of an item the children might like to buy, e.g. a toy car or teddy. Label it with a price tag. Discuss with the children how many pounds it might cost and choose a child to write the price on the board. Choose another child to count out a matching number of £1 coins. Check with the class.

Repeat for different items and prices.

# Section J: Picture maths

## J1 Picture the number

*To solve simple mathematical puzzles; to make simple predictions involving numbers*

Draw a picture on the board. Explain that it is a picture that gives clues about a particular number. For example, draw a square to represent '4', or a spider to represent '8', or a tricycle to represent '3'.

The children guess what number you are showing. You can be creative, and sometimes obscure!

## J2 Draw on me

*To solve simple mathematical puzzles; to make simple predictions involving numbers*

Choose two children. One stands with his back to the class, whilst the other 'draws' with a finger a number on his back. He has to guess what number it is – check the class agree.

Repeat.

## J3 Picture house

*To recite the number names to 10*
**Number line (1 to 6)**

Draw an outline of a house on the board. Choose a child to select a number from the line, e.g. 4. Draw four windows (for example) on the house, with the children counting as you draw. Another child chooses a different card (e.g. 3), and you draw three chimneys (for example).

Repeat for each number on the line.

Extend to numbers up to 10.

## 4 Window panes

*To recite the number names to 10*

Draw three windows on the board: one circular, one square and one triangular. Choose a child to say a number up to 10, and choose a window. Divide the window in the matching number of panes and count them with the class.

Ask different children to imagine something they might see through the window.

Repeat.

## 5 Birds in a tree

*To recite the number names to 10*

Use corners cut from envelopes to make small finger puppet birds. Each child should make one or two. Choose a child to stand at the front and be a 'tree', with arms and fingers outstretched. Choose a child and say One bird in the tree. They place a finger puppet on one of the 'tree's' branches (fingers). Choose a different child and say Two birds in the tree. They place a second finger puppet in the tree. Continue adding birds one at a time until there are ten.

Count them in unison with the class.

## 6 In between

*To suggest numbers which lie between two given numbers*

Draw three circles on the board. In the first draw four objects (e.g. four dogs). In the third draw six objects (e.g. six cats). Consult the class How many in this (the first) circle? Four. How many in this (the second) circle? Six. How many will go in the middle circle? Five.

Choose different children to draw fish in the middle circle, until there are five. Count them together. Write the numbers beside each circle.

Repeat for other 'in between' numbers.